BEAUTIFUL DREAM

Other books by Barry Cottrell:

The Way Beyond The Shaman: Birthing A New Earth Consciousness, O Books/Moon Books 2008

Entering Earth's Time: A Pleiadian Perspective for Planetary Awakening, published independently 2019

Sounding Eternity: Shamanic Incantations and the Poetics of Sonic Power, drivenLine 2021

BEAUTIFUL DREAM

A Poetics of Ecstasy

BARRY COTTRELL

drivenLine

First published in 2022 by driven*Line*
The Clock House, Widford,
Burford OX18 4DU
United Kingdom
www.drivenline.uk/beautiful_dream

ISBN: 978-1-7399205-3-1

The front cover image is *Totem*, linocut, 330 x 445mm by the author © Barry Cottrell
For Barry Cottrell's engravings inspired by these poems see www.drivenline.uk/beautiful_dream

CONTENTS

"…to move into a zone
of unintelligibility, the only
place where the possibility of
discovery lies, where the future
is not at the outset already a
thing of the past."
John Cage, *Musicage*

Introduction

The poems in this book may at times seem unintelligible, or at least difficult to understand. Yet in his essays on Dante, T.S. Eliot says that the task of the poet is to make people "comprehend the incomprehensible."[1] He argues that genuine poetry can communicate before it is understood and that "in good allegory… it is not necessary to understand the meaning first to enjoy the poetry."[2]

In his brilliant book, *Albion: The Origins of the English Imagination*, author and historian Peter Ackroyd discusses the intricacy and complexity of Anglo-Saxon verse emanating from Albion: "Out of this land of visions emerges a poetry of the dream-world….The dreamers of the tribe were highly praised because in their state of charmed sleep they were able to unite heaven and earth."[3]

Ackroyd views the great Anglo-Saxon poem, *Beowulf*, as being "in part a dream-poem; the strange elegies of the Anglo-Saxon spirit are enacted in unreal landscapes compounded of dream and vision."[4] He points out that the structure of the poem "represents the fascination with what is difficult, and the resistance to easy interpretation."[5] The same could be said of this book: *Beautiful Dream* is also a collection of allegorical dream-poems, imbued with qualities of strangeness, mystery and elusive interpretation.

While the brilliance of Anglo-Saxon verse shone in the West, at the same time in China under the Tang dynasty (618-907CE), monks in Mahāyāna Buddhist monasteries were practicing *dhāranī* incantations. *Dhāranīs* are strings of syllables, letters or words which are infused with spiritual power. Whether uttered as ritual speech-acts, or inscribed as text, they can be used as contemplative icons to help or protect others. As scholar Janet Gyatso points out: "...the significance and function of the text far exceeds its size and its denotation, since its primary purpose is not to describe but to engender or invoke a protective power."[6]

One form of *dhāranī* practice is the 'forbearance' *dhāranī* in which the 'object' signified is the Buddhist principle of emptiness. The practice reminds the practitioner of what has been forgotten, namely emptiness and birthlessness.

Quite often the strings of syllables in *dhāranīs* appear to be completely meaningless or nonsensical. Yet as scholar

Paul Copp has pointed out: "it was precisely the meaninglessness of the texts that made them so profound."[7]

Beautiful Dream also presents enigmatic strings of syllables uttered in what may sound at first like meaningless "cacophanies" or inscribed in "impenetrable thickets" of text. Yet, like *dhāranīs,* they may also be understood as encoded sound, as "contemplative icons"[8] with consecratory meaning which can only be 'grasped' by letting go of the attempt to understand or grasp them analytically.

This is a poetry of the dream-world that defies analysis. The form and expression of these poems is condensed and infused with a spiritual power born on a new octave of meaning. In pursuing each of these narratives to its unfolding mythological destination, the reader may take part in a lyrical celebration of the liturgical essence of human nature, and share in the rapture of expanded awareness.

References

1. T.S. Eliot, "A Talk on Dante." *The Kenyon Review*, Vol. 14, No. 2, The Dante Number (Spring, 1952):188.

2. T.S. Eliot, "Dante", *Selected Essays* (London: Faber and Faber, 1969):268.

3. P. Ackroyd, *Albion: The Origins of the English Imagination*, (London: Vintage Books, 2004): 49.

4. Ibid.

5. Ibid:25.

6.J.Gyatso,"Letter Magic: A Peircean perspective on the semiotics of Rdon Grub-Chen's Dhāranī Memory," in Janet Gyatso (ed.) *In the Mirror of Memory*, (Albany: SUNY Press, 1992):191.

7. P. Copp, "Anointing Phrases and Narrative Power: A Tang Buddhist Poetics of Incantation," *History of Religions*, Vol. 52, No. 2, Narrative and Incantation in Chinese Buddhism (November 2012):146.

8. Ibid:147.

The Deep Within (*Tractatus Physiologicus*)

Eels eyes sparkle
sooner relieved
than penetrating maybe
formless oceans
set within the stupefying
loneliness
of personal engendering
ricocheting through
mountain
valley
up through endless
possibilities
of half-sized
crowing platelets.

Reckless maiden
epiphanies of stone
extracted from pile-high
scenic lacing
where harvest-time
perpetuates this drop
in tempo
from oscillating rhythm

of posing,
and ha, ha, ha
the laugh comes last
when eels seek
raft-enhanced carnivals.

Syntax sighing with carnations
and low-strung perpetuals
intoxicate far-flung rituals–
havens for the poor and disabled
crucial to raiders
yet unproven as schemes
with hazy names.

Peace
hope
and love
of

The entrance is open
doors no longer slide
removed from their hinges
and left to grow old.

Enter.

Asking for the time–
precious letters opened
undisclosed treaties
have become the norm
licences to preach
the summer into oblivion.

Yet the instigator
continues to suck
the marrow from the bone
likening the act
to a harmony of the spheres
pretending that lower reaches
cannot empty buckets
full of dough unrisen.

Maybe in time
the torch resonates
with fire cracks.

And sarsasparilla taste
strengthens the heart
for poker dice
rolled

breaching terms unwritten
but so hard and fast
adhesive streaks
laying
reach under
to hold down any proclamation.

So loosen–
and sooner sprayed
with alchemical spray
transforming crops with laughter
humbling the cumulus–
no reproaches come closer
than any other master-
minded prayer.

Silver lode-stone tricks elixir
into medication for gall stones
unaware of the po-faced reproach
from heavenly sliding
slipped discs crunched
into the pay-roll
of half-baked settlers
whose armaments reason
the posterior notion
of locating

hey, hey, locating
hey, hey, jewels
impressario
within the stump.

Sooner ruptures come
straight down the line
and embarkation
of anal location
simply strikes
the emblematic time
until low knows
the most.

Flancia Flinchman

Flancia Flinchman
was with her ancestors
starting to pour the contents
of her brightly shining feathers
into the summer-time of her life
honing in choruses
waiting to favour the graces.

And as she tied her cord
tighter around the rim
of her velvet bride's bag
holidays sane and sensual
came into the vein.

Post strike,
but no-one dared to lay down
the heaviness of the plover's tread.

She saw into places which
darkly safe
could nor-westerly be sheened
by the bright breeze
shifted and spilling the races
from mid-ocean wave.

Ordinarily the trumpet blew
to give notice of the time for rising
yet without sound
only movement could wrestle signs
from the patient frozenness.

Flancia Flinchman
came into each room
of her father's house
son et lumière
excreting from the sky
hoping to unload heaven's breath
trying to maintain
local pieces of roasted pork.

Salad days are forever splendid.
Streaking between the bone
cleft in stone
the striking lance shafts
sharp into the place
penetrating.

And she looked into the glass jar
dark with starlit night
and softened the treasuries

of peace-making rodents
crafting their lairs
sorely missing
the pleasures of daylight
crumbling gruff truffles
from the burrowed entrance
to the underworld.

And Flancia Flinchman came
and divested all her jewellery
and flames expired in the process
of becoming–
rake's process.

The Muzak Of The Spheres

Presenting arms
asking hard-boiled questions
trading the possibility
that sometime in the near future
this prophesy comes true.

Cardboard profile
lifting the paved
gilded
foremost castle.

He who cups the hands
into the sign
of post-trended pillage
comes silently down the passage
into a place
where only lip-service prevails.

Crazy line tip-toeing
over faces lifted high
and circumambulating.

Soaked residues
bask in the sun
and steam rises
to encrust and desiccate.

Heavenly tremble
seeing all the convolutions
in the process of baking bread.

Brittle
so broken
task sharded into the many lifes
of harvest time
as the seed bursts.

Dancing in the moonlight
crying out for more
than can possibly be contained
in this pauper's place
yet instrumental in coping
with endless rapture.

Tip-toeing again
this time into the prism
shafting light

eyes beaming
reeking of only-just-cut-up-in-time
as wafting and waiting
the jasmine rode lanes
of purple porphyry
trancing lies
as they ricochet off walls
of imprisonment
into traces of embolism.

Rogue playing dice with devices
draining the life-force –
kitchen richer than at possibly
any time in the past
for the meal is so nearly ready
consummation of so many times
when you came so close
and inched your way to breathing
towards the light of day –
raising the tenor
shifting rhythms
placing the point in its rightful place
so that the melody comes in tune –
proof of that planetary quest
beyond the trophies
of wrecked high-life.

"Inquire not into the truth
of the many layers
as each has its own inquisition"
nor begging the question
un-pasting signs
which raked those eyes with lies
of eking out an existence
when so much more
was available and offered
unconditionally tainted with bliss.

Proof rocks the minds of many
linked to the quest
and narrows the scope
of panoramic inquiries
when time twisted the rafters
and the scope was narrowed.

High light the muzak of the spheres
when lifting the light rifted
on crass rackets
of laden strikes
and pork-encrusted lakes
crying blight crimes
against humanity's appetite
for frozen food

blasting the roof-top open
so that the rain comes in soddenly.

Pinhole vision
prime-time for cooking the waste
into a tasty meal.
"Suffer the little children
to come emptily"
poste-haste
in case incarcerated prayers
are left to muffle the cries
of open-ended pleasure.

"Seek ye not the praise of emperors."
Treasure the quiff
and the nigh-ripe lick of trees' fruit.

Umbrage coated with resin
soft-seamed lichen prefaces
the whole universal trip
down the tide-line
so that in the morning light
you see that only in make-believe
is the trouble fully composed.

Pay the rent.

Beautiful Dream (Hump The Rogue)

Po-faced and Cupid bow
strikes the heart of the matter.

Can you see what is happening
to the rodents in the gutter
as they crowder for hungry-
pointed lacing,
when treatments fail
and they seek the most rough-
edged solution?

Sighing all the time
mind is eclipsed
by stony traces
of embraced carnage,
humbler sensitivities
tread through canopies
which have lowered
to protect empty braces
of seed-like supplements.

Indigo raiment
umbrellas can often take

your so right places
of hopeful harnesses
seeking the triumphant populace
as they raunch their way
to ink-stained strikes.

Pondering the question –
po-faced again
rook-like
over colossal heaps
of broken-down
Tables of Numerical.

Do you find a place here?
Seer, prophet –
seems unprofitable.

Energies not wasted
entry into that light cavern
of proof that dusty canyons
can contain the secrets
of every loaded device
which sits uncomplained-at
frozen in time
between processes of leeching

and ride like Rock of Ages
roasting.

Pride enters the equation
between keys of lock-broken exits.

Have enough of this –
soak up the residue
hold on to social laughter rasped
as the creak of excrement
is reeking.

Beautiful dream
serene drifter
cars are crossing the bridge now
over the tidal flow.

Need to excrete –
exhale the viper
exhale the effluence of aeons.

Princely income
no exit here –
hold the time of your life
and hump the rogue
as he wrestles with aching bones.

The Carmelites' Rebellion

I

Undistinguishable from tokens
of previous salutations –
in other words,
the greetings faded from auguries
which had been constructed
in order to pose questions
and elicit answers
to pressing engagements.

Hard-earned pennies melted
under the gaze of solar epiphanies
while green enablement
pictured squires and ladies
promenading
through furrowed pastures
after the flood had made mud
of their land-locked love.

Half humping the rogue again
for this time he's fallen down
the lane side and broken his leg,
standing now at half-mast

hungry for vitamin supplements
to boost the precious tonnage.

And the monks were surly
for in the crocus garden
the worm had turned
and eaten lettuce, spinach
and all the fine beautifully-tended veg.

And so their silence was astonishing
as half the populace stormed
their rich-picking place
to open up the gates
and let in fresher air,
prayers priceless still
but parsimonious in the extreme.

And porphyry again
wrenching the sacred emblem
from their grasp
as if to say
that no more could be extracted
from their deity.

But their prayers went heard
into the star-lit sky
imploding the vestry
in the process,
for their power was too great
to handle safely.

And in that last quiet moment,
they sank to their knees
and wept into the soil
as their tears turned
to deep carnations
and others to irises
paler petunias
and their garden sparkled
with the incandescence
of their weeping
as they lay there exhausted
yet sleeping so peacefully.

II

Within the carmine reservoirs
floated fish in visions

sepulchral grating,
yet still they floated in visions
hunted for aeons
but now peaceful passengers
in the gently undulating liquor
of post-natal streams
as sight startled them into picturing
and also into postulating
their purpose
their prose hinting always
that crying out louder
could produce goods
which are less stereotyped
in their region.

In the carmine lake
the fish blew bubbles
which picked their way to the surface
and popped in the air
releasing ventriloquism odours
of literary wafting platelets.

And as these pockets of airlessness
circumnavigated entrances
to the rogue's palace
the astonishing miasmic

pleasure of inhalation
stupefied and tamed
nuggets of aurum
and plenty of crow-flying fauna.

Huguenots would have known
their presence
and the task of humbling
the controllers of crops –
hash-traps catalysing
stunned pools
of ectomorphs swimming,
needing to pay buoyancy tithes
in perpetuity.

Honest patience –
cryptic trip switch
until electrifying forces
shatter the crowing platelets.

Harmony in parcels
yoke loaded and presented
as if the norm.

Studently plover fly nigh the time
for caressing the carmine lake.

Trials And Tribes

Cyclamen protects half-moon radiance
embedded within
form-enhanced rituals,
and the palette changes –
striations blend on the cusp
with holy night and raucous dawn.

Sincere illusions painted in the sky
enter visionary reliefs
carved in stone
lacking only the portrait
of heart and soul
as bliss strikes hard
on the unknown warrior.

Contemplative explorations
led to unveiled archipelagos
which breathed new breezes
into the open place
where hiding in the thicket
we went down
before roosting
in the privately-laced umbilical.

Foretold in populated tales
the wrist revolved
around the door-knob
until wrenching cryations
placed too much pressure
on the door-step
so that craft sank
and the mighty rose
from halls of fame-inflamed praise.

And the parson
pleasured himself.

Tendencies To Tremble

Carcinogenic –
climbing closer
to the praise-worthy stem
tides far lower than ever before,
fire in the breath staunches wounds
cauterizing veins
unholy smokers unredeemed
yet divinely satyrizing
all the playhouses
within the helping domain.

Carcinogenic –
even carnivorous yet prayed upon
when bright starlit skies implode
and posture the tasks unmastered
under stormier sighs
harder to grasp.

Carcinogenic –
yet free from emblems
leaf from a page
pressed with encyclopaedic

massive broken tome
crumbled to dust,
and under the glow-worm's
incandescence
there comes frigidly struck
the tendency to tremble.

Proofs Of Entrails (Biological Substrata)

Slow down paved passages
wet night prevails
and the story opens
so much sooner than expected,
canal miasmic troughs
seeming to question
the prairies' shrub-like
scrotum-located truths
divested of garments
strewn over flower-beds,
time for so many more tricks
like staff rooting
the electrolytic lair.

Each time
the odour wafts across
stamen and juice
lucky that no other possible way
can stimulate this pride
many times miasmic,
the caught seeds pray for release
and heavier weights load the dice
until no chance remains

for the prize taken unquestioningly
handsome yet flawed in the grain –
has striations
claim proof of entry
so much lower
than in the charted terrains
of yoke-loaded preferences –
singularities
sonic yet roasted.

Half past the time
to emblemize simple stitches
which weave together
the plover and the wave,
truth upstart incandescent
yet rafted to a place
of great eminence–
hilarity beyond words
and all the time these traces
are being made
there's no question
that in the hallway
in the dark corner
there lurks the triumphant gnome.

Scattered all over the terrace
corpuscular crickets leaping to and fro
studiously remembering
their chequered path
until the in-breath takes more
than it can hold and
explosions rift the pensive concrete
stolen from the mill grist.

And in the time of fright
the tendency to seizure–
strontium holistic craft–
there is no other main route to follow
than the carpet-bagged rack
of amazing graces.

Funky tulips hold an essence
which leaches into the atmosphere
as if none knew before
the prosaic catalyst of its sip.

Hundred upon thousand
hardened trome
stratospheric secrets
aching to be revealed
and healing the postnatal shock

of effigies animated
into starkly enhanced laughter
as the sage seeks solitude.
And open days laced with presence
culminate in aeons of references
to porphyry as the prime suspect,
singing songs of dark night
undertows prosaic load
of emasculated pyrogenic mentors.

So soon
in the blinking of an eye
the wider pride shoots like a star
into the base and root
of each biological incarnated
master of disguise
and tokens steeped in perfume
breeze through those corridors
high-minded
and sutured to the heaving
breathing chest,
only then rising
from the maiden flower
incense of best few luminescences.

And the tenderest in kept.

The Brazier And The Bush

Trading the newly-
developed technology
for praise and hunger subsiding,
lip-smacked oregano
plays with trees and plants
and the bush too livens the landscape
preferably too short
for posing in the scrub.

Heathens subside
into postnatal crying and laughter,
overtures to succinct
melodic pressure,
and hymns from the night lessen
the previously-owned quarters
so that in the room
the girl sat
half-naked
yet completely embalmed
in the smoke from her candle.

And outside the brazier burns stubble
and auguries omit the idea
that sometime soon
large parts of the picture will crumble
as the bush shoots out.

Son Et Lumière

Cracks defy temptation
into trespass upon vainglorious
treacheries of hope
and radiant scratches
when neon
corpuscular fires
lit the skin.

And in those times
the weight became unsupportable
and the serpent struck so hard
at the granite base
that effigies crumbled
into sparking pyrogenic
streaks of screeching.

And many times
there re-emerged the love of Earth,
balmy skies warmed by the sun
and loaded with ether.

Crenellations–built strapping castles
in grotto-like forests,

and humping the old rogue
he limped his way past the cave
sat down and shook himself
with grief-tones.

And as porphyry extruded
into the night,
black light leeched
into the stream
so that water came silken
with the sheen
of dappled darkness,
and the black river emptied
into the ocean stream
where deep-sea creatures
licked their way
through the feast of entropy
and under the sea bed crept
half-engendered hopes of renewal
which screeched their way
to the surface
and erupted into the sky
where hurricanes hungered
for their potency
and Earth disemboweled its hora–

the times of its life–
to meet the treaties
brought from far away
in the blinking of an eye.

And those roasted days crept
into the story
of forgotten dreams
plagued by the trembling
of the hand
manual dexterity,
prisoner to the task.

So close came rasping craftsmen
to the bone
that emblematic crosses
cut through preaching
and marked the spot
where hard-plastered roses lay
relieved of their perfume.

And suddenly
the moment merges
with the wind of change
from solar sources.

Emblematic Of Estevan

Scorched earth and stark contrast
between wave and shore
the time came for frayed edges
to be mended and stunningly striking
in their embellishment.

Estevan stood ten feet tall
cloaked in night
the glow so strong within
and he sailed
to the shore of porphyry
looking around and about
essential strewn lilies
making the enclosed lake
sacred for his song.

He opened wide his mouth
and cried signs of hymns and tokens
which scattered around
the landscape of his dream
setting into stone the posture lost
and power deceived
in locations to the west.

His purpose was to stoke the fire
of cracks in the terrain
so that the shrieking
would subside
through peaceful places
re-enchanted after the fall
from graceful atavism.

And so he planted
all those seeds of memory
in porous places
as the sigh finally left him
speechless for posterity
until these times breathe
the canal of vital stock back
flowing into his havens
of emphatic juice-words.

Now comes the quizzical treatment
assembling multitudes
into the single sound
recapturing the potency
of wisdom-bliss
humbled by the aeons
of emblematic rhyming

between cords
of harp-linked resonances.

And Estevan shot through the sky
mind out of time
with reasonableness
until notes sang
and he saw the entrance
back into his places
inhabited now
by moments left untouched.

Time To Dine

If the time to dine came
earlier than expected,
mercurial strips of ether
would waft across the table
enveloping guests
and no roast would appear.

For in the timing of the meal
lies the secret of its nourishment.

A ghostly *frisson* plays
around the room
the stench of ectoplasm
retched from shores of cardiac arrest
seemingly pleased about the profit
made from tasks
enslaved upon the populace
and the troll only made it tamer.

So come dine on time
for history can now reveal
the imploded vestry
caught in the vial
harboured by a virgin.

Closer To Home

The stark hard truth melts
into seasonal greetings
as prize-winning tales endlessly told
in gamin form
lurch the seed-thought
through empty space
into soil partly tended
yet prosaically studied
by scholarly minds
right on the mark
chosen for their hilarity beyond words
composed darkly yet intimate
in their lent cross-hatched tone.

Ardvaark the perennial flight
higher now than the slipstream
crossing oceans
of sylph-engendered sky
coming through to meet populations
stranded for a while
waiting for their release.

Lonely plover stalking,
keeping wise
within the humourless brogue
and undertaking new ways of leaving.

Story-tellers again seeing
and believing
the market-driven pleasures
open-ended in their ecstasy
ravaged by cumulative bench-marks
notched and hammered into place.

Simultaneous transitions
lodestone half-past the time
for reversing the roles
magnetised by delight.
And then they came
in greater numbers than before
pleading for dismemberment
of the host.

Closer to home sits the rich
in situation-specific
knowing enclosure,
rowing perhaps against the tide

with wider deeper oar-strokes
finding the vein of gold
in the midst of the river.

Perhaps the proof comes
when underneath the seat
the cat sleeps
and the post is opened
to reveal an invitation
written by hand
in Rosicrucian ink
and parting from the incidental
tithes no longer in demand
the freer hand-shake
and warm embrace
looks like welcoming back
to known parties
communally distinct
strewn with emblems
of disenchantment,
ridden on.

And so comes the return
to open-plan consciousness
doors dismantled

breath entering all spaces,
disclosed and undisclosed
populated and emphatic
verdant and sparse.

And in that inhalation
comes the breeze sweetly relieved.

The Bowman Bends His Steel

Painful penetration
shrinks the will
to be easy
in physical presentation
and underneath the briar
lies curled the mammal
struck down by mute sensation.

In the sky fly
ark-like ravens
coasting downwind
until passed over
by hurrying cumulus masses.

And the bowman bends his steel
for his arched recklessness tenses
until the poignant posture
stretches into elastic fright
that the shot might misfire
and the destination be missed
unaware, of course,
that the bow bends only

when the time is right
and nowhere can be off the mark
for—in itself—
the action makes light
the pressures of doom-laden
shocks of wrong.

The bowman bends his steel
braced to kill time
as miasmic pleasure
creeps up the spine
tingling every nerve
into latent wakefulness
waiting for the moment
when the ritual space of the body
bursts into chorus of celebration
that can only mean
memory has become
extinct in the membrane
and only now is time passing.

The bowman bends his steel
fraught yet aching
for the ancient origin of archery
in its pristine streak
of marking the end.

And over and over again
temperatures rise
mercurial elixir feeds the feast
of hailed arch-enemies
who kiss each other
on the lips
and know their purpose
of the posture adopted
in those times.

Peeling away the skin
fruit lays bare its juices
virtuoso lip slipping
into cinquefoil trips
down plane tree avenues
of dusty heat
and the song remained
poised in the wind
blowing through the leaves
until the rustle
mystified
all forms of life
which were dormant
as they shrieked awake
and screeched their delight

of hoping-to-see-more-now-
than-ever-before.

The bowman bends his steel
unencumbered now
the simple arched back
radiating heat.

Who Are The Poor People?

Porphyry presents us
with the ingredient
for locating distant shores at night.

Signs strike time embellished
with the engrossing thicket
since reams of tasks
pile high and roam the sky
until the time takes nine-to-five.

Righteousness links
to the roving reporter
as links are made
between the eco-task
and poor people.

Who are the poor people?
Stroding down the lane - triff
strings of lacing pyres
burn the blackness into skies
etched with red ochre orange streaks.

And underneath the proven scales
are trenches of like-minded truths.

Intimate But Not Extinct

I

Why should anyone consider the
possibility of emptying the stream
into a desert to be a viable solution
to the drying up of abundance?
Why not pray for rain?

Carp hard in the precincts
of emptying
soaked in the residue
of prayed lanes
simply treacherous
convolutions of reich.

Hum-drum cases seem to
puke in the sewer
tip-toeing along.

Prolonged prefects wrench particles
of loaded weight from hardened stone
reaching simply stressed
soothing hum-drum.

Crenellations of proof
by the night air
hemmed in to the enclosure
havens of imploded rust
from street lights
and gates
and fences
where the spikes
and the hedges
have protected horrible processes
of accumulation.

Green grow the rushes O.

Rowing down the river
towing the line behind
the roving postman
seen treading the path
down Highgate Cemetery
past the rich and famous
down through the central dome
parking inside systems
of perforating petulance.

Kind eyes lend grace
to the impact of rented
traces of oblivion
so that nothing goes beyond
the places where it was intended
to erect monuments
to shroud the garden in cement.

And on he went down south side bank
and opened up the roof
to amaze everyone who stood
and looked out to the sky
and high-rised
that endless populations had streamed
through the same place
and noticed only progress
nonetheless.

And so the prefect turned back
into his tent
to strip naked and raid the ark
before the presentation
of public money,
so that crimes could be paid for
and laid down

in exactly the right place
for their opening ceremonies.

And when the time had come
for moving into stranger raiments
then they dressed in cardboard
packaged.

So soon the shift comes
from the strobe-light
which flicks
and the moment is over
and the mind is in the panoramic.
So soon the memory fails
and out of the corridor
came the tribe of demented sailors
and suffocating preachers
from expansion and contraction
to expansion and contraction
heaving the need
in those roasted days.
Presentations soon came forward
for their testimony
as time trails away behind the ox.

Hundreds, even thousands,
even millions of coughs and sighs
fill the skies expectorating
leaving untouched the truce
which was made before
the rooster exploded.

Humble.

II

Intimate but not extinct
for the varying tones of the screen
layer the denizens
of drenched diamonds.

Honing in on the process
of encapsulation
hiding under the train
of precious crystal
magnetizing memories
in the flux of
trace-like embraces.

Symphonies strike a chord
of umbrage
so that the half-rendered pride
climbs slowly through the thicket,
and detecting no more summer love
the end comes quickly
while over the hill
birds fly brightly
into the dark sky.

So slowly
so going through this process
can be a very stabilizing
night owl's protection
rather than the strewn roof
full with pockets of right and wrong
hidden in the beams
slating and shifting
all through the night.

People come to this place so rarely
because it's not seen to be safe.
Yet let it go
for safety is a mirage

of comfortable contracts
rather than abandonment
of the veneer
seen through treason-like right
and penetrating prospects
strum and ring
through those skies
where the archipelagos vaporized
so many aeons ago
that there is mere seeming
empty space now.

Rushing along
tragedy hides in the thicket
heart cries delight
when the pra....pra....

Tonnage and attachments
array radius sofa-bred.
Reedles of imagination
sooth-like
yet promiscuous in the extreme
when the hopes
of all those weary souls
were dashed on the rocks
of rough justice.

Pancreatic.

Pummelled to death
yet reinstated
as the flat flamingo.
Home on the range
trickling like a light-hearted
trend of expectorant.

O ecflightation ingest the bud.
Run ford before the flood
of humbler residues.
Rick lach
slow-lo-lo-lo-lo
the boat.
How, how, how
hiya, hiya, hiya....
Rice and crafted raiders
hoof, hoof, hum.
Ranting, rhyming
ark in archipelago
flamingo.
Roafing, roafing, roafing.

The Lonely Planet

Catastrophic fall
not knowing that the embargo
has been lifted.

Plaintiff seeks redress.

Standing at the edge of the lawn
an abyss of tidiness
encroaching crater-like
into the wild places,
hundred upon thousand
of broken down stones
litter the passage
from history's niceties
to tomb-like posterity
as the gently undulating liquor
continues its seeping flow
through the cracks and crevices
of monuments
insinuating that thought is liquid
when the vapour has become
too dense.

And prize-giving time
lurks in the wings
for possibilities of roast
the unharnessed vengeance
burns away
at the corpse
of the formerly-known pride,
lanced and then devolved
into statuesque similarity
to the pole which maintains
the so-called dignity of states.

And signs simply stretch the senses
until snapped and recalled for service.

Deeper in the distance
hoards of mongoloid hun
rampage down time's cul-de-sac
until the music stops
and they all sit down bewildered
all layered into place
until the cock crows
and awakening bears fruit
in the priestly enclave.

Stitched into the picture
the web
formerly redundant
now embraced
reseaming the lonely planet.

Providence

Blowing briskly along lanes
breezes steeped in ether
readiness praise the salient
roll of canopies
which hold place over
indented terrains
and the influx of stark
last calls reach down
to precious metals
within Earth's layers
and saying that creatures
cannot see the high tide coming
is presentiment to unfurl the past
steeped in the rich liquor
of savoured tempestuous
cadences riding high
so clearly beyond the plain
yet pulling behind a ton
of netted radiance.

The pleasures of enticement
accumulate in the chest
and locked away as treasure

until noon-time comes
and all convene for the opening.

Providence personified
in perpetuity
as clove stitched
in the blanket
and seeming to waft
as lace and eyes
spy the highest particle
of porphyry's trade.
And children lick their fingers
when eager for the sweet
vestige of heated meetings
of substance circulated
only in the tub of sighing
home seeing loaded knowledge
of empathic nurturing
and parsimonious interests
in carted lasting parcels
of emperors' raiments
which are no longer required.

Perfection and indigo beauty
sail through the porous path
towards infiltration

into praying monks
so that jewels sparkle
in the dark
and the tangent tricks goals
from their consummation
sparking righteousness
into trembling
on the edge of the curb
unable to cross the road.

And Providence herself
listens to the barking calf
and lies low in the mournful
coast lines with moaning
mist-filled holes—
collagraphed patience
hand engraved shame
as the pistol snaps sharp
through the glass-lined
presence of turquoise
names held and depleting
their conscience to breath-
taking horary times
conspicuously open
to the prevailing winds
laughing the ghastly harvest

into proven tables
hedging their bets
that if only they can hold on
to the rituals
then all the schemes hatched
in nebulous stained beds
will profit the mesmerised idol
curiously steaming up
as ho-ha the last laugh
passes the craft work.

Renegades always praise
starving patriarchs
as if they were the norm
turned round and elevated
onto the stage
in which each precious
private plate
is served up with nothing
except the source.

And underneath the table
is consumed the real meal
half past midnight
but "better late than never"

never-known unholy stokers
still keeping coal burning
on the raging fire
and menacing ridiculous
postures straight down the line
Hades sisters and brothers
lake-lovers
pressed steel stitches
keeping them together.

And another consummation
takes place
as clocks stop
batteries expire
and the power is imploded—
reading the meter
becomes impossible
without a magnifying glass.

Heaven has turned into spent
questions and melted into
eternity's embrace
ever loading the brace
pillows puffed for comfort
and ready for preferably
requests for peaceful breath

as the sighs subside
and the breeze gently rises
so that in between there is
a moment of astonishment
as meeting unbelief ceases.

Hail many parochial preachers
in all their exalted manes
of clairvoyant praise.

And the gaze ahead
and the outstretched hand
accepting the gift
stringent conditions were placed
on this special relationship
until no-one bore more abundance
than the presidents of republics
ingrained in the bone
and no-one could see
the pressure placed on privacy
until the fire burned from within
and forced an evacuation
to a homestead imbued
with heart's blood pulse
and warmth of cherished taste—
nothing ever wasted.

The Sincerity Of The Peace

"We seek," you say,
so times change
and undulating wave-form media
carry the sonic stream
of emphatic verdance
towards its manifestation.

For the priorities claim their victims
and need to be side-stepped
if only for the blinking of an eye
so that presentations are made
from within
and the soaked template of ennui
cracks dried as an emblem
of roasting heat.

Seen from the juncture between form
and sinuous streaming aid
no floating fish come into this lake
all is alive and strumming the rhythm
rauchously driven
sane yet stitched in a zig-zag pattern
for the tokens of heavenly pleasures

come slowly
and if only they would speed up
the nuclear fears would dissolve.

And as that time tests
the sincerity of the peace
then only waiting
will meet the needs
not endlessly
but as if in an emporium
blown and struck
striking time.

Dragon Blood

"Ether-sifted salient features
dawn in mists
from future conquests
where no blood is spilled
no creature dies"
and dragon blood passes through
treaties between ancient enemies
enriching the fix
and stealing the acrimony
from their lips.

For none is wiser
after the prison doors falls
unless they open their eyes.

And the layers of
clan-engendered sediments
wash away the tidal flow
leaving hardly a trace.

The Troll[1] Of Animated Treifs[2]

Both silent
and rauchous
emptying
persuasive
simultaneous transitions
from euphemism
to truth.

Present trends
encapsulate
the loff[3] focused
of the essences
which stream
through your process
of enablement.

Pai, pai, pai, pike
pike arise
in the lesser streams

---

[1] Troll: a song of which the parts are sung in succession, to chant merrily (1575)

[2] Treif: literally 'torn apart' - food that is deemed unkosher (forbidden under Jewish law)

[3] Loff: laugh & cough simultaneously

full of loaded sailors
half-mast
for the so-rasp sake
half-mast only,
holding down the corners
of the stencilled papers
into communal perspectives
trials and errors made
from policed camion
holding within
the straightened pictures
of energized praise
and computed raid on the jeweller
hovering inside the *kudos*
of folds with half-pasted
trading, havens within
the straight and narrow
lanes of place
and holding on to the prayer
which has been caught
on the hop
handed down
and passed through
the souvenir shop
out into communal
races.

Sympathetic operations
suddenly restrain
from sending down the lies
within the packages
of rodent-like
pulverised steam.

Carriage and tender trip
through old-visored
sensual treatment.

Who could have possibly imagined
that this could have come to pass
before stoves of plaintiffs burn
with the troll of animated treifs?

Half-mast
for the straightened edge.
Half-mast
for the *kudos* rampaging on
down plains
of lichen-grown praise.

Higher energies rise up
and electrify the raucous parties
of enema-raw floating stuff.

Please see that all the contained
effluent is processed
before you recycle concepts
from future drainage.

Hymns through the night
slight, upright
fading on the flow
as the tide turns.
Traders betrayed
raiders berated.

Pew-like preferences
simple in solitude
soaking religion
through pores impacted
under aeons
of corpuscular prayer.

Knighted.

Under currents stray
through the foreign-
plastered radiance
cutting
tremulous

even if the only seeming
Portuguese man-of-war
preys on the particles
which have sunk
to a seriously low level
of embodiment.

Ark adrift on the tide
of contagious fortune
hoping for a new resolution.

Impish risk
when all that can be seen
is the nose
in front of one's head
instead of passages
through *kudos*
and emerging triumphant
on the other side.

Bit-mapped
parsimonious
ruling each tidy mind
concentrating hardly
on the paymaster.

Acronyms screech
their prayer
as the dust settled
over the new parquet floor.

Unruled
unlined
unstoppered,
encephalic creations
postulating brain waves.

From the heart
there seems to come
the racing pulse
towards which ever enemy
needs to be seen
face on.

Over-duned sand
falls through the cleft
within the crack
as emptying under the face
which tells no tale.

Roofbeam and open day
lusting for deeper

drenched concatenation
hybrid toes
uff,
affronted by
parsimonious.

Game
set
no match
point taken
to the limit
unspoken
heaving over the proof
as falling
and caving in
to entropic revision
scrutinized unendly.

Hope born
with no eyes
all surprise
no demise
bliss arise
the size of
universal
preference.

Epilogue (Forest Of Dean)

Picking my way
through the Forest of Dean
and the presence
and past tension
of carbon fired
the reservoirs' practice
of honing the instincts
as preambles for cutlery
dropped embargoes
upon hedgerows
perforated drum-
skins standing in line
underneath wet posts
simulating pretty pictures.

And the laziest of the members
fell off his chair asleep.

Creeping along floorboards
scratched with stylistic emblems
of nominal employees
and the flag staff
vocalizes in colour

the steaming prison
pressurized vegetables
hundreds of them
where the sense of waste
sinks the boat
yet within the dream
undercurrent comes
signs that all is not lost
since precious jewels
float in this medium.

Back on dry land
cumulative frequencies
make noise grating so too-
scratchingly sharp
harnesses snap
and the pilot bales out
free falling.

Then comes the rain
situating the best
kind of token in perpetuity
legendary status forms
with the craft
and once disassembled

plays only one tune
over and over
and over
and over.

www.ingramcontent.com/pod-product-compliance
Lightning Source LLC
Chambersburg PA
CBHW050505120526
44589CB00047B/2415
* 9 7 8 1 7 3 9 9 2 0 5 3 1 *